SILLY SYDNEY

Written By Shane Alvares   Illustrations by Ana Patankar

Silly Sydney

Written and Created by Shane Alvares

Illustrated by Ana Patankar

Publication date January 2016
Printed by CreateSpace

ISBN-13:
978-1519782755

ISBN-10:
1519782756

With Gratitude

Mom – I payed attention

Carrie – I pay attention

Dylan, Sydney and Brayden – I'm paying attention

Inspired by and dedicated to my incredible family

Carrie-Anne, Dylan, Sydney and Brayden.

THIS IS MY BIG SISTER DYLAN

WE LOVE DOLLS AND STICKERS
SHE IS REALLY GOOD AT CRAFTS

AND ONE DAY I'LL BE
AS GOOD AS HER

WE LOVE PLAYING TOGETHER ...

... MOST OF THE TIME.

THAT'S BRAYDEN

HE'S MY BABY BROTHER

HE LOVES MY HUGS AND KISSES!

I TEACH HIM
HOW TO SHARE

AND
PLAY
GAMES

AND HE JUST LAUGHS!

SORRY
I'M SO SILLY DADDY.
I'LL BE A GOOD GIRL ...

"OH SYDNEY,
MOMMY AND DADDY
LOVE EVERYTHING
ABOUT YOU...

...THAT'S WHAT
MAKES YOU OUR **SILLY SYDNEY**"

Message from the Author:

Everyday life in North America is busy for most people and we are no exception, which is why I decided to write this particular story. As a father of three children all under 6 years old, and a registered Early Childhood Educator, I have a keen awareness of the struggles and pressure this adds to all families.

My goal is to inspire parents and caregivers alike to become more present to all children as they find their place in life. I hope to specifically educate and inspire fathers to become more PROACTIVE in the lives of their children and discover the power that lies within these relationships.

Finally, I wish to inspire my children to strive for greatness in all areas of life. This book is my legacy that you can carry with you for the rest of your life as proof that when I taught you that "you can be, do and have ANYTHING you desire", that I also took the ACTION to create this for myself.

With love and gratitude,

Shane Alvares

5% of all profits will be donated to HandFull Hearts (www.handfullhearts.com), a non-profit organization helping families in the Greater Toronto Area. Fabiana & Stelios, you have impacted my life more than you know! Thank you and I love you.

I would like to extend my deepest gratitude to the people
who have helped me create this book.

Ana and Mukul, I honestly could not have completed this with anyone else.
Not only were you both incredible on a professional level, but I just felt our synergy
was perfect. Mukul, thank you for helping me with every last detail, answering all of my
questions (no matter how late I asked them!!) and being so supportive. Ana, you
captured the essence of my family with your illustrations. Some things I provided
the background, but on others it seemed like you were tapped into our energy.
I am forever grateful.

Rick and Judy, you've been a gift from God for me. I don't have many words that can
accurately describe the feeling of love and gratitude I have for you both. You have
absolutely changed my life from the moment I met you.
I am forever grateful. I love you both.

To all of my grandparents who made the descision to come to Canada back in the 1970s.
It took two families with an unselfish vision to create the fruit that I have created
with this book. I am grateful beyond words for my life and opportunities that come
with it here in Canada. I love you all. Thank you.

Thank you mom for raising me with a bit of both old and new school parenting! If you
weren't so open minded and progressive in raising me, I would not have had the
fortitude to pursue this. I love you.

To my wife, Carrie-Anne. Thank you for being by my side all these years. You've definitely made the journey exciting and worthwhile. We have three beautiful children. Thank you for everything. I love you.

Dylan, Sydney and Brayden, you are my greatest gift and blessing! You have opened my heart in a way I could never have imagined possible. It is with this love that I created this book. Since the day Dylan was born, my goal was to be the greatest father possible in every way. I've realized over the last 5 years that neither money nor gifts matter in the eyes of a child. It's my time, rather my presence, which is the greatest gift I have to offer you. I'm not just talking about just being present in your lives, but being present to your lives.

This book is my legacy that I leave for you. I could be like every other well intentioned parent and advise you that you can be ANYTHING and achieve ANYTHING you want in this life. I could tell you to work for yourself and do all of these great things. That would be doing a good job as a parent. But I decided a long time ago that I was not going to be a good parent; I am a GREAT parent! So instead of just telling you, I decided to also show you and do it myself. Keep this book as a physical reminder that when daddy says you can be, do and have ANYTHING you want, that he also did the same! I wish you a GREAT life! I love you all beyond any words I could ever write.

"No matter where I go, no matter what I achieve, no matter who I become, my greatest success is being 'daddy'".

Love Daddy

Please use the following pages to create your personal memories with your children. Have them write down their favorite part of the book, draw family portraits or just create whatever comes to their mind and be present with them in these next few pages!